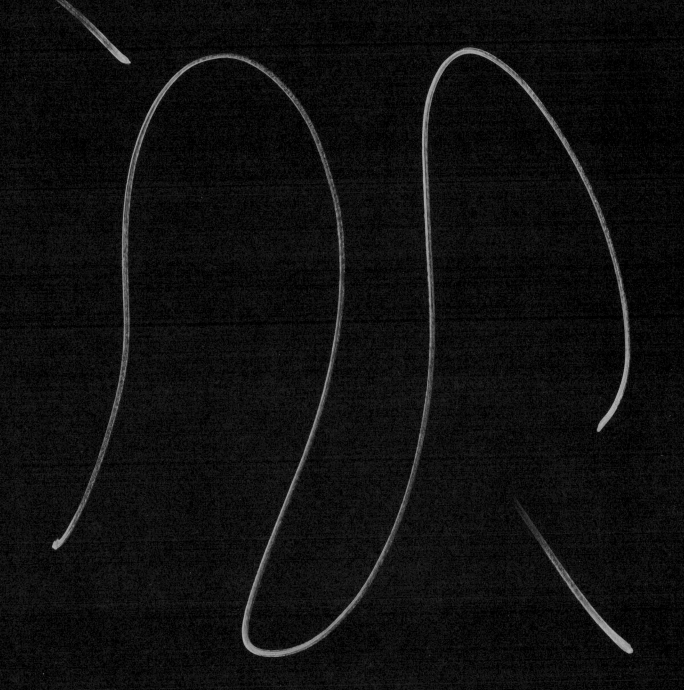

pandama**N**ia

Washington, D.C.

GOVERNMENT OF THE DISTRICT OF COLUMBIA
D.C. COMMISSION ON THE ARTS AND HUMANITIES

Mayor Anthony A. Williams

D.C. Commission on the Arts and Humanities
Dorothy Pierce McSweeny, Chair
Anthony Gittens, Executive Director
Alexandra MacMaster, Project Coordinator
Yann Doignon, Program Associate

Commissioners
Félix Ángel
Clara R. Apodaca
Jane Lipton Cafritz
Lou Durden
Cathy James Ehrman
Jay Gates
Isabella Gelletich
Derek Gordon
George Koch
B. Warren Lane
Ethelbert Miller
Franklin Odo
Maurice Shorter
Gertrude Saleh
David Umansky
Gail Berry West
Monica Wroblewski

D.C. Commission on the Arts and Humanities
410 Eighth Street, N.W., Fifth Floor, Washington, D.C. 20004
Phone: (202) 724-5613
TDD: (202) 727-3148
Fax: (202) 727-4135
Web: www.capaccess.org/dccah

pandamania

D.C. Commission on the Arts and Humanities

ORANGE FRAZER *PRESS*
Wilmington, Ohio

ISBN 1-882203-44-5
Copyright 2004 by D.C. Commission on the Arts and Humanities

Additional copies of *PandaMania: Washington, D.C.* may be ordered directly from:

Orange Frazer Press
P.O. Box 214
Wilmington OH 45177

Telephone 1.800.852.9332 for price and shipping information.
Website: www.orangefrazer.com

Writer: Michael McBride
Photographer: John Woo
Editor: Anthony Gittens
Book and Cover Design: Jeff Fulwiler
PandaMania Title Design: Crabtree + Company

Library of Congress Control Number: 2004112151

andaMania Launch

In the photo at PandaMania Launch Ceremony at the National Zoo are pandas "William Shakesbeare" and "Red Pandagon" flanked from right to left: Artist, Jiashan Mu; Chinese Ambassador, Yang Jiechi; Mayor of the District of Columbia, Anthony A. Williams; Shakespearian actor, Ted Van Griethuysen; Director of the National Zoo, Lucy Spellman; President & CEO, World Wildlife Fund, Kathryn S. Fuller; Chair, D.C. Commission on the Arts and Humanities, Dorothy Pierce McSweeny and Executive Director, D.C. Commission on the Arts and Humanities, Anthony Gittens.

Writer
Michael McBride

Photographer
John Woo

Editor
Anthony Gittens

Project Chair
Dorothy Pierce McSweeny

Project Coordinator
Alexandra MacMaster

Program Associate
Yann Doignon

Communications
August, Lang & Husak, Inc.
Crabtree + Company
Fleishman Hillard
Greenfield/Belser

The D.C. Commission on the Arts and Humanities dedicates the PandaMania exhibition and book to the artists who through their participation in the project have done so much to enrich the cultural life of our great city.

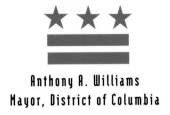

Anthony A. Williams
Mayor, District of Columbia

Greetings from the Mayor

PANDAMANIA HAS HIT THE STREETS OF WASHINGTON. Our colorful friends are everywhere you turn—street corners, Metro stops, parks and neighborhoods. They are here for you to photograph and enjoy, as much as we enjoy bringing them to you.

There is a new vitality in our city. Washington is alive with art, theaters, museums and galleries. Our neighborhoods bustle with restaurants, shops and unique charm. As you discover PandaMania, you will also discover a city filled with wonder and surprise. We welcome you and look forward to seeing you again and again.

Anthony A. Williams
Mayor, District of Columbia

PandaMania
Washington, D.C.

WHEN THE D.C. COMMISSION ON THE ARTS AND HUMANITIES decided to create a second citywide public art project, after the hugely successful Party Animals in 2002, which featured donkeys and elephants, the choice of the giant pandas was a natural given the phenomenal popularity of pandas among Washingtonians. Thus was the birth of PandaMania. Using lessons learned from Party Animals, the Commission purchased 150 blank panda sculptures and called upon artists to bring them to life with their imagination and creativity.

PandaMania highlights the extraordinary talents of a special group of very talented artists, students and teachers who participated in the project. This wonderful collection of public sculpture has brought smiles and spontaneous fun to the streets of Washington (where taking things a bit too seriously is the order of the day). PandaMania culminates with an auction during which the D.C. Arts Commission will auction the panda sculptures to the public. All proceeds from the auction will help fund arts grants and arts education programs.

Washingtonians have had a love affair with giant pandas since the arrival of Ling-Ling and Hsing-Hsing at the National Zoo in 1972. Though Ling-Ling and Hsing-Hsing have passed on from old age, the National Zoo continues to engage new generations of panda lovers with Tian Tian and Mei Xiang. During the first eight months of their arrival at the National Zoo in 2000, Tian Tian and Mei Xiang became instant celebrities, attracting an astonishing two million visitors. Visitors to the Zoo's Panda House quickly realize that these cuddly creatures have an uncanny ability to draw people into their world. Whether they are methodically munching on bamboo, contently sprawled on their favorite boulder, or enthralled in one of their frisky antics, pandas remind us of the joys of everyday life and the importance of just having fun.

This comprehensive book contains photographs of all 150 PandaMania sculptures, interesting information about giant pandas and fun facts about those memorable creatures that all too briefly inhabited the streets of Washington during the spring and summer of 2004.

A LOVING PANDA

Artist: **Ernesto Leon**
Sponsor & Location: **Lombardi
Comprehensive Cancer Center at
Georgetown University Hospital**

BEARRA COTTA WARRIOR

Artist: **Melissa Shatto**
Sponsor: **The Coca-Cola Company**
Location: **Rizik's**

Inspired by the discovery of thousands of life-size terra-cotta soldiers in China, Melissa Shatto created "Bearra Cotta Warrior." The ancient Chinese sculptures were installed to guard the tomb of China's first Emperor, Qin Shihuangdi. The statues were accidentally discovered in 1974 by workers digging in a well.

CHOCOLATE DIPPED STRAWBEARY

Artist: **Debbie Smith Mezzetta**
Sponsor & Location: **Caribou Coffee**

A descendent of two generations of candy makers, artist Debbie Smith Mezzetta, created "Chocolate Dipped StrawBeary" to pay homage to her "rich" family history. "StrawBeary" weighs the equivalent of 3,000 chocolate-dipped strawberries.

ACCESSORIES ARE WHAT SEPARATES US FROM THE ANIMALS

Artist: **Chad Alan and his Friends**
Sponsor & Location: **Tiny Jewel Box**

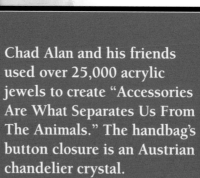

Chad Alan and his friends used over 25,000 acrylic jewels to create "Accessories Are What Separates Us From The Animals." The handbag's button closure is an Austrian chandelier crystal.

Artist Lynda Andrews-Barry created "Freedom Panda" based on the 1855 sculpture that crowns the U.S. Capitol Building. The sculpture, titled "Freedom, Triumphant in War and Peace," is by Thomas Crawford. Crawford's original design included a "freedom cap" which was given to slaves upon their release, but objections from a Confederate general prompted Crawford to replace the cap with a Native American headdress.

FREEDOM PANDA

Artist: **Lynda Andrews-Barry**
Sponsor: **McCormick & Schmick's
Seafood Restaurant and M & S Grill**
Location: **Marriott Wardman Park Hotel**

APPLE PANDAWDY

Artist: **Nancy Nahm**
Sponsor & Location: **Whole Foods Market**

PANDA IN TIGER'S CLOTHING

Artist: **Dinah Myers-Schroeder**
Location: CPB

APPLE PANDAWDY

Artist: **Nancy Nahm**
Sponsor & Location: **Whole Foods Market**

PANDA IN TIGER'S CLOTHING

Artist: **Dinah Myers-Schroeder**
Location: CPB

PANDELA ANDERSON

Artist: **Maggie O'Neill**
Sponsor & Location: **Café Milano**

ZEN PANDA

Artist: **Suzanne Pender**
Sponsor & Location: **National Archives**

TEN THOUSAND HAPPINESS

Artist: **Jiashan Mu**
Sponsor & Location: **The Embassy of
the People's Republic of China**

17

ARTHUR PANDRAGON

Artist: **Katherine Kahn**
Sponsor: **American University**
Location: **American University Washington College of Law**

PATCH PANDA

Artist: **Carien Quiroga**
Sponsor & Location: **The Shops at 2000 Pennsylvania Avenue**

South African artist Carien Quiroga created "Patch Panda" using recycled materials stitched together to represent the restorative effects of healing the natural environment. The recycled aluminum printing plates attached to the sculpture are from the artist's native country. The artist used over 10 pounds of crochet copper wire and 400 pieces of stitched aluminum.

LING-LING IN THE SKY
WITH DIAMONDS

Artists: **The Maverick Group with Lucinda
Crabtree, Bonnie Fitzgerald,
Karol Forsbert, Sylvia Leftwich,
Carol Talkov and Friends**
Sponsor: **Willard Associates**
Location: **Willard Inter-Continental Hotel**

PANDA MELON

Artist: **Anthea Zeltzman**
Location: **21 & I Streets, NW**

BAGGY BEAR

Artist: **Robert Alston**
Sponsor: **The Museum of Bags**
Location: **Sette Osteria**

POPPY PANDA

Artist: **Roberta Marovelli**
Sponsor & Location: **Banana Café**

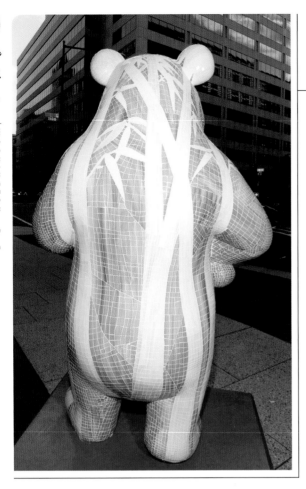

THE TALE OF THE BAMBOO CUTTER

Artist: **Nina Fuerth**
Location: **Barnes & Noble Booksellers**

BOOTED

Artist: **Francisco Quintanilla**
Location: **Metro Center Metro Station**

There are 221 Washington, D.C. parking tickets painted on "Booted" by Francisco Quintanilla. The Denver Boot is made of polyurethane-coated wood. The artist does not currently own a car and reports that he was never booted when he had a car (so he says).

25

BOOGIE WOOGIE PANDA
Artist: **Nathan Welch**
Sponsor: **Mr. & Mrs. Richard England**
Location: **International Square**

CAREFREE PANDA
Artist: **Bob Wilder**
Location: **Mazza Gallerie Mall**

JAZZ-E PANDA
Artist: **Greg Scott**
Sponsor & Location: **Café Milano**

D.C. TREE PANDA
Artist: **Margery Goldberg**
Sponsor & Location: **City Museum of Washington, D.C.**

EMPEROR P'ING

Artist: **Mary Fran Miklitsch**
Sponsor & Location: **Mandarin Oriental,**
Washington, D.C.

A Long Love Affair

In 1972, U.S. President Richard M. Nixon made a historic visit to the People's Republic of China to help improve relations between the United States and China. As a gesture of friendship, China promised to send a pair of giant pandas to the United States. There are an estimated 1,000 remaining wild giant pandas scattered throughout central China making giant pandas one of the most endangered species in the world. After months of heavy lobbying by the nation's zoos, President Nixon decided, given the pandas were a gift to the people of the United States, the National Zoo would be the most befitting home for Ling-Ling and Hsing-Hsing.

The arrival of Ling-Ling and Hsing-Hsing in the U.S. ignited American's fascination with pandas that continues to this day. China's gift to the U.S. enjoyed a long celebrated life as icons of peace and conservation. Ling-Ling died of old age in 1992. Her mate, Hsing-Hsing died in 1999. Ling-Ling and Hsing-Hsing did not successfully breed during their years in captivity, leaving the Nation's capital without a resident panda until the arrival of Mei Xiang and Tian Tian in 2000. Mei Xiang and Tian Tian are ten-year loans from China to the National Zoo. Continuing the legacy of their predecessors, Mei Xiang and Tian Tian receive an astonishing 7,000 visitors per day.

STARS & STRIPES

Artist: **Christine Miller**
Sponsor: **Interstate Worldwide Relocation**
Location: **US Navy Memorial**

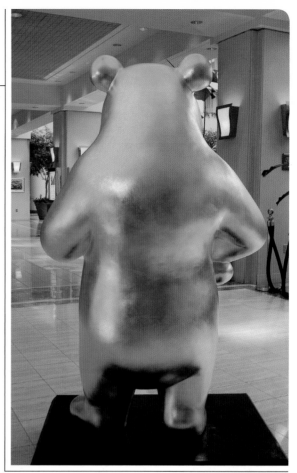

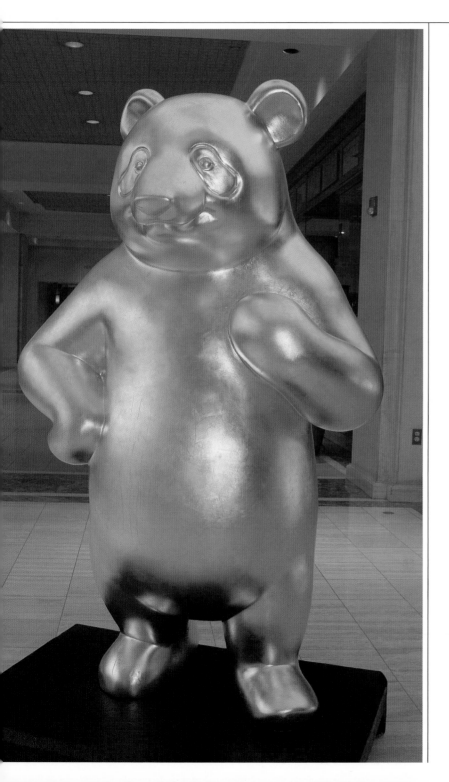

PANDAGOLD

Artist: **Gilded by Joseph Youss Kadri, Master Gilder**
Sponsor & Location: **Grand Hyatt Washington Hotel**

Gilding is the "Art de Vivre" for Master Gilder, Joseph Youss Kadri. His "PandaGold" is gilded using 1,700 individually applied 23.75-carat small feather-weight gold leaf squares.

PANORAMA PANDA

Artist: **Lisa Foucart**
Location: **Folger Theatre**

CIRCUS PANDA

Artist: **Claudia McElvaney**
Location: **Borders Books**

Artist Claudia McElvaney who created "Circus Panda" says she did not intend to create a masterpiece, but was determined to make smiles.

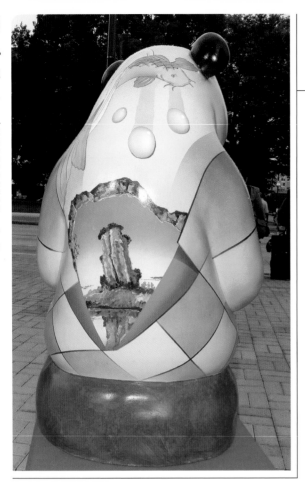

EAST-WEST

Artist: **Byron Peck**
Location: **Washington Convention Center Authority**

MONUMENTAL REFLECTIONS

Artist: **Marsha Stein**
Location: **D.C. Visitors Center at Reagan Building**

AMERICA'S CHILDREN VI

Artist: **Carol Spils**
Sponsor: **Calvert**
Location: **One Judiciary Square**

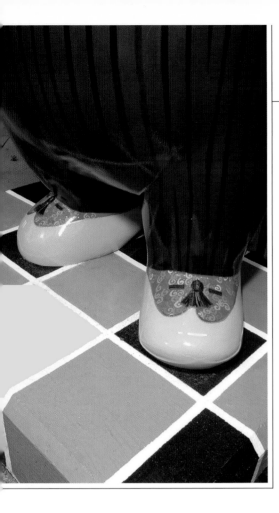

PANDA OF THE OPERA

Artist: **Mary Howe Kiraly**
Sponsor: **Café Milano**
Location: **Sette Osteria**

BEAR NAKED LADIES

Artist: **Patapsco High School and Center for the Arts**
Location: **Newark Street & Connecticut Avenue, NW**

PAISLEY PANDA

Artist: **Laura Traverso**
Location: **1225 13th Street, NW**

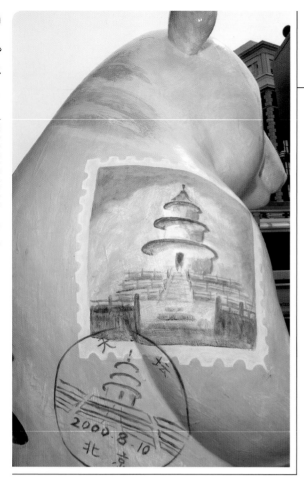

" 'JIA' "家, HOME"

Artist: **Penghua Zhu**
Sponsor & Location: **National Postal
Museum**

CHERRYBOB

Artist: **Laurette Kovary**
Location: **Cosi Sandwich Bar**

MY SACRED LAND

Artist: **Karlisima.com**
Sponsor & Location: **PEPCO**

DANCING BEAR, "THE GOLDEN ROAD TO UNLIMITED DEVOTION"

Artist: **Jonathan West**
Sponsor & Location: **Caribou Coffee**

THE FLOTSAM OF PLAY

Artist: **Chuck Baxter**
Sponsor: **Waterfront Associates LLC**
Location: **Waterside Mall**

Nicknamed "Flotsy" by artist Chuck Baxter, "The Flostsam of Play" contains several thousand objects found in alleys, on streets and playgrounds in his Shaw neighborhood since 1993. The artist reports that he still has enough found objects to cover at least two more pandas.

BEARRING FRUIT

Artists: **Kate Nagle**
Location: **White House Visitors Center**

WHERE'S PANDA?

Artist: **Alexander Overby**
Sponsor & Location: **The Shops at 2000
Pennsylvania Avenue**

FOR A LIVING PLANET

Artist: **David Ciommo**
Sponsor & Location: **World Wildlife Fund**

The surface of "For A Living Planet" created by David Ciommo contains every land mass on Earth. The puzzle pieces represent areas of the world that have benefited from World Wildlife Fund conservation efforts. The two missing pieces represent areas still in need of conservation. The World Wildlife Fund adopted the giant panda as its official logo in 1961.

47

TAI-SHANDA

Artist: **Michael Vain**
Sponsor: **Dorothy and Bill McSweeny**
Location: **The John F. Kennedy Center for the Performing Arts**

THE GIANT PANDARUS

Artist: **Gus Garcia**
Sponsor: **HECHT'S**
Location: **City Museum of Washington, D.C.**

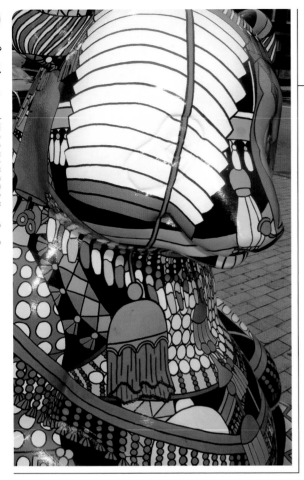

MIKE'S CARPET SHOP

Artist: **Katerina Barry**
Location: **Eastern Market Metro Station**

Katerina Barry 2004

RUSTY

Artist: **Howard Connelly**
Location: **1735 New York Avenue, NW**

WILLIAM SHAKESBEARE

Artist: **The Shakespeare Theatre Costume Shop**
Sponsor: **Metropolitan Washington Airports Authority**
Location: **Ronald Reagan Washington National Airport**

"William Shakesbeare" wears a period costume similar to his inspiration, William Shakespeare. It took a team of 19 artisans, using 45 yards of fabric, over 232 yards of trim and gallons upon gallons of polyurethane and varnish to create his costume. For the record, Shakesbeare's measurements include a mammoth 54" neck, 70" chest, 75" waist with a surprising 4" inseam.

ALL THE WORLD'S A STAGE

PRESIDENTIAL PANDA

Artist: **Michael Rigsbee**
Sponsor & Location: **National Museum of American History**

TI-BET YOUR LIFE

Artist: **Catherine Hillis**
Sponsor: **Golden Triangle BID, Corp.**
Location: **Dupont Circle Metro Station**

Who's buried in Grant's tomb?

A Giant Project for a Giant Bear

WITH THE HUGE SUCCESS OF PARTY ANIMALS, the D.C. Arts Commission learned a great deal about organizing large-scale citywide public art projects. Party Animals featured donkey and elephant sculptures representing American icons. When the Commission decided to organize a new large public art project, it wanted to use another animal as a canvas for creativity and expression. Selecting an animal that had captured the hearts and minds of Washingtonians was not difficult given the phenomenal popularity of giant pandas in the District, and the Nation.

After the D.C. Arts Commission chose the giant panda for the project, the Commission went about the business of organizing, promoting and garnering support for the project it called PandaMania. Party Animals had created many friends in the business, diplomatic and local communities who enthusiastically embraced plans for PandaMania. The D.C. Arts Commission contracted with TivoliToo in Minneapolis to fabricate 150 blank panda forms in two poses, one standing and the other sitting on a boulder. The standing panda is 5½ feet tall. The sitting panda is 4½ feet tall. Attached to their cement bases, both sculptures weigh a whooping 750 pounds.

The Commission announced the opportunity to participate in PandaMania by mailing over 10,000 calls to artists and by emailing another 5,000. Artists from around the country submitted over 1,300 design proposals. Artists living in other countries, including Brazil, France, Columbia and China also submitted proposals. The Commission organized a selection committee, representing diverse areas of expertise, to review the proposals. The Commission provided selected artists with an honorarium to create their designs on the blank panda sculptures—then the real work of PandaMania began.

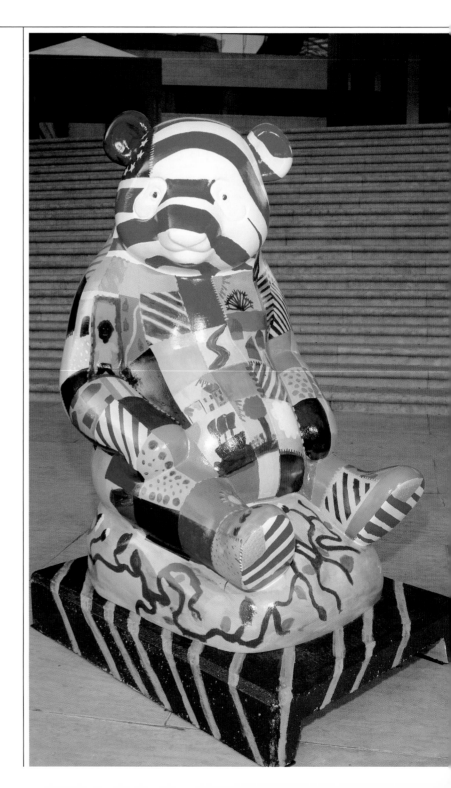

UNDERGROUND RAILROAD

Artist: **Janney Elementary School Students**
Sponsor & Location: **The Embassy of Canada**

CRO-MAGNON PANDA

Artist: **Anne Currie**
Location: **California Pizza Kitchen**

RAIL FENCE PANDA

Artist: **Mary Beth Bellah**
Location: **Rhode Island Avenue Metro Station**

"Rail Fence Panda" by Mary Beth Bellah refers to a block-style quilt pattern. The sculpture's cover is a genuine quilt as it contains three layers of stitched fiber. The artist used over 125 different fabric designs to create the quilt.

58

URBAN PORTLY

Artist: **Nick Aumiller**
Location: **Georgia Avenue-Petworth Metro Station**

COIN PANDA

Artist: **Dakota Warren**
Sponsor & Location: **Inter-American Development Bank Cultural Center**

Artist Dakota Warren used over 3,000 wooden circles to create "Coin Panda." The circles were fabricated in California and transported in a large suitcase to Washington before being individually sanded, painted and applied to the sculpture.

WRIGHT PANDA

Artist: **Allan Gow**
Sponsor: **Interstate Worldwide Relocation**
Location: **Ronald Reagan Washington National Airport**

Inspired by the original Wright Brothers Flyer, the "Wright Panda" by Allan Gow, uses structural steel to support its wings. Converting the mammal into a machine tripled the size and weight of the original sculpture.

THE SIDI BOUQUET

Artist: **Margaret Dowell**

Sponsor & Location: **The Washington Post**

The Washington Post

Artist Margaret Dowell created the colorful coat of "The Sidi Bouquet Panda" by finger painting. A fall left the artist temporarily without the use of her hands and arms. Unable to use a brush but still determined to participate in the project, she used her fingertips to paint the sculpture.

61

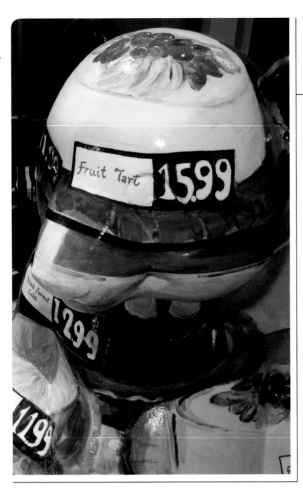

PANDA CAFÉ

Artist: **Joan Oshinsky**
Sponsor & Location: **Caribou Coffee**

CROUCHING TIGER HIDDEN PANDA

Artist: **Cindy Brandt**
Location: **D.C. Department of Recreation**

The surface of "Crouching Tiger Hidden Panda" by Cindy Brandt is a jelly bean-like camouflage that hides 32 little pandas.

PANDOMINIUM, THE BIRD SANCTUARY

Artist: **Maribeth Blonski**
Sponsor & Location: **City Museum of Washington, D.C.**

PANDA L'ENFANT

Artist: **Kid Power-D.C.**
Sponsor & Location: **D.C. Chamber of Commerce**

...udents at Kid Power-D.C. created "Panda L'Enfant" to honor Pierre L'Enfant, the original designer of the Federal City. The ...oject not only provided the students with ...lessons about art but, also lessons about ...olitics when the students discovered that Andrew Ellicott and Benjamin Banneker actually completed the city's design because of a falling-out between L'Enfant and patrons of the project.

TIME 4 LOVE

Artist: **Luis Peralta**
Location: **JW Marriott Hotel**
Pennsylvania Avenue

PAPILLON BEAR

Artists: **Robert Dixon-Gumm**
Sponsor: **The Adams National Bank**
Location: **The Investment Building**

PANDAbandana

Artist: **Marsha Lewis**
Location: **Mr. Henry's Restaurant**

The design proposal for "PandaBandana" by Marsha Lewis was conceived and delivered to the Arts Commission within 24 hours of the proposal deadline. After her design was selected she and a friend drove to and from Connecticut, 6 hours each way, in a Saturn (yes, a Saturn) to pick-up and deliver her painted panda.

SAVE HABITAT NOW

Artist: **Kay Jackson**
Sponsor: **Capital Hotel and Suites/**
St. Gregory Hotel and Governor's
House Hotel
Location: **Governor's House Hotel**

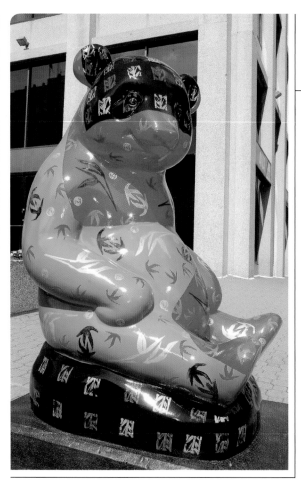

YOU ARE WHAT YOU EAT

Artist: **Leslie A. Cohen**
Location: **1101 16th Street, NW**

PUR-R-R-FECT PANDA!

Artist: **Jody Wright**
Location: **Francis Scott Key Memorial Park**

"Pur-r-r-fect Panda!" by Jody Wright contains portraits of cats adopted from no-kill animal shelters.

71

SNOWFLAKES

Artist: **Shirley Koller**
Location: **Juanita E. Thornton
Public Library**

DREAMTIME WALKABOUT

Artist: **Kyle & Barbara Bancroft**
Location: **Riggs Bank**

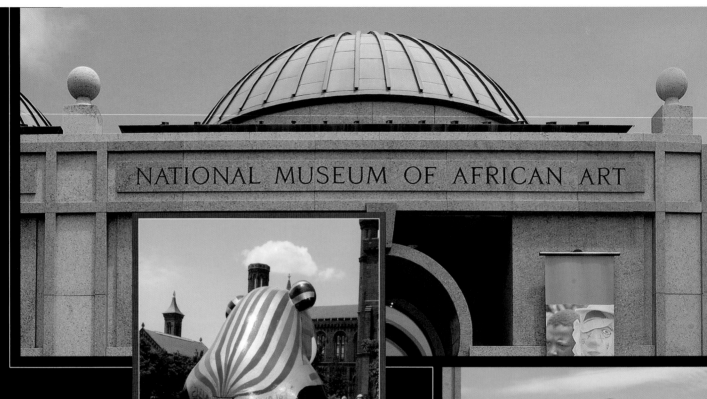

NATIONAL MUSEUM OF AFRICAN ART

CLEOPANDRA

Artist: **Millennium Mind/
James Cunningham**
Sponsor & Location: **National Museum of
African Art, Smithsonian Haupt Garden**

PANDA-UNDER-CONSTRUCTION

Artist: **Michael William Kirby**
Sponsor: **Fannie Mae Foundation**
Location: **National Building Museum**

A Panda-Personal: "Panda-Under-Construction" by Michael Kirby seeks "Pandela Anderson" by Maggie O'Neill. Michael reports that in the middle of his panda is a pot of gold (don't believe it "Pandela" or Maggie, we checked).

PANDEETAH

Artist: Joe McKenna
Location: Courtyard Marriott-Embassy Row

Artist Joe McKenna who created "Pandeetah" uses his own unique brand of conservation by artfully interbreeding a panda with a cheetah. The artist reports that his hybrid species would certainly be more adaptable than its forebears.

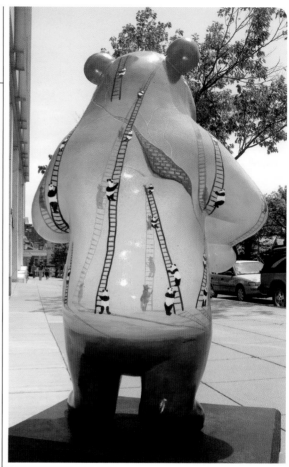

CLIMBING PANDAS

Artist: **Zora Janosova**
Location: **Universal North Building**

IMAGINING LANDSCAPE PANDA

Artist: **Kimberly Thorpe**
Sponsor: **The Washington Times**
Location: **Evening Star Building**

BEAR TO THE BONE

Artist: **Justin Jackson**
Sponsor: **Clark Construction**
Location: **Bank of America**

ROBOPANDA

Artist: **Michael Nathan**
Sponsor: **Crabtree + Company**
Location: **American Chemical Society**

PANDY WARHOL

Artist: **Margaret Finch**
Sponsor: **Mandarin Oriental,
Washington, D.C.**
Location: **Smithsonian Arts &
Industries Building**

DIRECTIONS

Artist: **Alden Phelps**
Sponsor: **Metropolitan Washington Airports Authority**
Location: **Ronald Reagan Washington National Airport**

CHINA DOLL

Artist: **Amy Goodstine &
Brandon Bloch**
Location: **Warner Theatre**

PANDA TALES

Artist: **Maret School Students**
Sponsor & Location: **Anacostia Museum**

PANDANCER

Artist: **Pamela Wilde**
Sponsor: **McCormick & Schmick's Seafood Restaurant and M & S Grill**
Location: **M & S Grill**

All wrapped in music—can you guess what song by John Stafford Smith "Pandancer" by Pamela Wilde is imagining as he dances?

SIGHTSEEING—D.C. STYLE

Artist: **Beth Baldwin**
Sponsor: **Fleishman Hillard, Inc.**
Location: **Political Americana**

Not Just a
Black-and-White Affair

AS ARTISTS DEVELOPED THEIR PROPOSALS, they saw the blank PandaMania sculptures as giant canvases to celebrate their creativity, to be inventive and to say something about Washington. Consequently, the Arts Commission received many compelling and technically challenging proposals with a variety of interesting themes and unique fabrication techniques—it was clear at this point that PandaMania was not going to be a black-and-white affair.

Many of the design submissions selected by the PandaMania Selection Committee proposed altering or eliminating the panda's black-and-white patch pattern, applying images or designs on the sculptures and using bright or unusual color palettes. Several proposals required altering the sculptural forms of the pandas by reconfiguring their basic shape or adding appendages. Applying mosaics, coins, fabric, photographs and other materials to the sculptures was also popular among artists.

The artists who participated in PandaMania clearly pushed the limits of what the Commission thought was possible. Their creativity resulted in a stunning, thought-provoking collection of sculptures bringing unexpected color, instant smiles and spontaneous conversation to the streets of Washington, D.C.

YIN-YANG

Artist: **Connie Slack**
Sponsor & Location: **Smithsonian's National
Zoological Park**

PRINCE PANDA

Artist: **Joseph Barbaccia**
Sponsor: **HECHT'S**
Location: **HECHT'S at Metro Center**

LAISSEZ LE BON TEMPS ROULER

Artist: **Eileen Cave**
Sponsor: **Fiduciary Counselors Inc./
Irish Channel**
Location: **Irish Channel Restaurant & Pub**

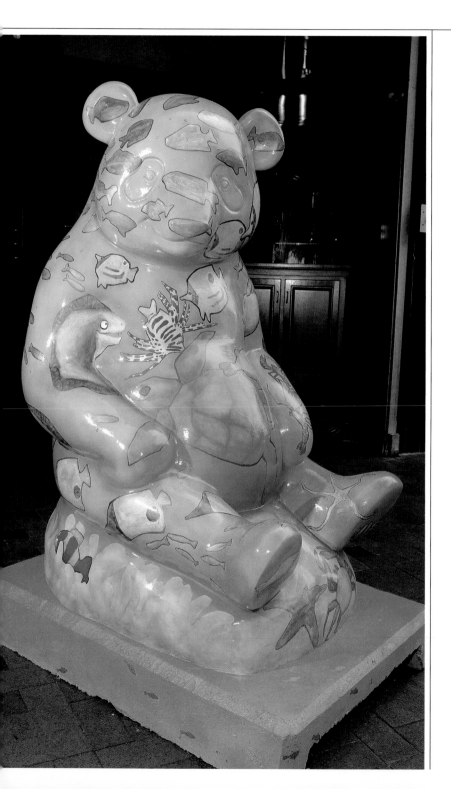

PANDAQUARIUM

Artist: **Naomi Campbell**
Sponsors: **McCormick & Schmick's Seafood Restaurant and M & S Grill**
Location: **McCormick & Schmick's Seafood Restaurant**

PANDAmania
Artist: **Olivier Dupeyron**
Location: **Farragut North Metro Station**

THE GREATEST GENERATION

Artist: **Zora Janosova**
Location: **American Red Cross**

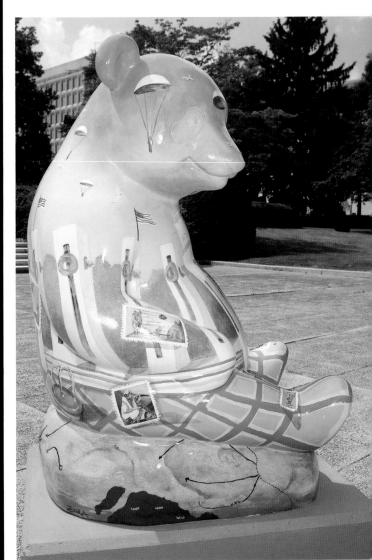

SHANG BEAR

Artist: **Dorothy Fix**
Location: **McPherson Square Metro Station**

PATRIOT PANDA

Artist: **Tom Kozar**
Sponsor: **Patton Boggs, LLP**
Location: **2700 M Street, NW**

YEAR OF THE PANDA

Artist: **Nicholas Shi**
Location: **Reeves Municipal Center**

PANDALUSIA

Artist: **Varvara Tourniaire**
Location: **Long & Foster Realtors**

"Kung Pao Panda" by Barbara and William Gordon uses a children's wading pool to create their bear's noodle dish. The noodles are made of 75 feet of plastic plumbing tube. The sauce is made of polyurethane and the chopsticks are made of wooden molding. "Kung Pao's" transformation resulted in a 50-pound weight-gain above his original size.

KUNG PAO PANDA

Artists: **Barbara & William Gordon**
Location: **Farragut West Metro Station**

LILY ROSE

Artist: **Lillian Perry**
Sponsor: **Kerley Signs**
Location: **DAR Constitution Hall**

At age 83, Lillian Perry is the most senior PandaMania artist. She has had copyist privileges at the National Gallery of Art for the past 43 years. Her panda, "Lily-Rose" was inspired by the John Singer Sargent painting, "Carnation Lily-Lily Rose."

HOME RULES

Artist: **Anne Marchand**
Sponsor & Location: **Washington, D.C.
Convention and Tourism Corporation**

THREATENED SPECIES

Artist: **Rufus Toomey**
Sponsor & Location: **Occidental Restaurant**

All of the plants and animals on
"Threatened Species" by Rufus Toomey
are on the endangered species lists of the
IUNC or the World Wildlife Fund.

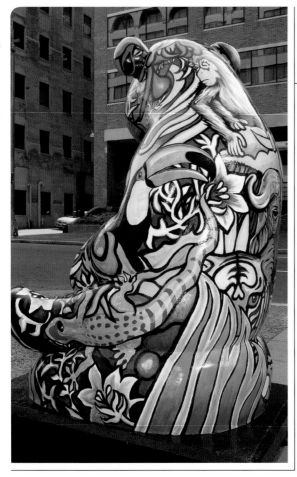

TRUE TREASURE

Artist: **Brett King**
Sponsor & Location: **Washington Marriott**

PHOSPHORESCENT PANDA

Artist: **Johannah Sloop**
Location: **Presidential Building**

BEARS IN SPACE

Artists: **Millennium Mind**
Sponsor & Location: **National Air and Space Museum**

PANDA TERRA

Artist: **Washington International School Students**
Sponsor: **Palette/The Madison Hotel**

"Panda Terra," created by students at
Washington International School (WIS),
contains 91 flags representing the
nationalities of WIS families.

Fun Facts
Serving Size: 1 bear
Unlimited servings
NO Calories
Totally fat-free fun
*Percentage of daily
value (DV) is based
on a standard attitude
of frivolity.

Raspbearry Jam   150 lbs. (68,038.8555g)

Amount/Serving	%DV*
Total Fat – 0g	0%
Total Carb – 0g	0%
Sugars – a gazillion g's	(tons of that stuff)
Totally Silly	100%
Total Fun	100%
Pro teens	(yeah, we're for them too!)

INGREDIENTS:
POLYURETHANE,
FOAM INSULATION,
STEEL TUBING, CEMENT
ACRYLIC PAINT, VARNISH
TENDER-LOVING-CARE

BEST WHEN
PURCHASED BY:
MAY2004

NO
RE
FRIG
ER
A
TION NECESSARY

Visit our panda for delicious fun,
hard-to-find hilarity, and
great outdoor activity!

whatwillwedo.redraspbearry.4fun

PEANUT BUTTER & RASPBEARRY

Artist: **Marygrace Antkowski**
Location: **Mazza Gallerie Mall**

The UPC code on "Peanut Butter and Raspbearry" by Marygrace Antkowski contains a secret message to the artist's husband, Michael (we didn't pry). The lid on "Rasphy" is made of a plastic flowerpot saucer. A mathematician had to calculate the panda's weight in grams for the label.

THE PANDA OF DAY AND NIGHT

Artist: **Maria Quezada**
Location: **Arena Stage**

WORLD WIDE PANDA

Artist: **Tyrone (Tipy) Taylor**
Sponsor: **America Online, Inc.,**
Location: **Mazza Gallerie Mall**

SUNSET PANDA

Artist: **Jeff Huntington**
Location: **Studio Theatre**

RED PANDAGON

Artist: **Claire Kuang**
Sponsor: **Greenfield Belser, Ltd**
Location: **Wachovia Bank**

PANDULUM

Artist: **Sean Younis**
Sponsor: **Calvert**
Location: **The Shops at 2000 Pennsylvania Avenue**

PANDRAGON II

Artist: **Cynthia Baush**
Sponsor & Location: **Kinkead's, An American Brasserie Restaurant**

PANDRAGON I

Artist: **Tita Rutledge**
Sponsor: **Design Cuisine**
Location: **Dupont Circle Metro Station**

THE LAST SAMURAI PANDA

Artist: **Mary Stasek Johnson**
Sponsor: **Clyde's Restaurant Group**
Location: **Old Ebbit Grill**

PANDILLUSION

Artist: **Emily Tellez**
Sponsor: **August, Lang & Husak, Inc.**
Location: **Boone & Sons**

D.C.'S CHOO-CHOO

Artist: **Claude Andaloro**
Location: **Metro Center Metro Station**

OCEAN SNACK

Artists: **Bell Multicultural High School Students**
Sponsor: **Fannie Mae Foundation**
Location: **Anacostia Metro Station**

PANDA VAN GOGH

Artist: **Kevin Richardson**
Sponsor: **Mr. & Mrs. Calvin Cafritz**
Location: **National Gallery of Art**

PERENNIAL PANDA

Artists: **John Bledsoe**
Sponsor: **D.C. Marriott & Renaissance Hotels**
Location: **Marriott Wardman Park Hotel**

WILL YOU MISS US?

Artist: **Jeannette Murphy**
Location: **Woodley Park-Zoo/Adams Morgan Metro Station**

A Colorful Breeding Ground

WATERFRONT ASSOCIATES PROVIDED THE ARTS COMMISSION with vacant rental space in the Waterside Mall in southwest Washington to use as the official PandaMania studio. Though artists generally prefer to work in isolation, and some did create their pandas in their studios, PandaMania provided many participating artists the opportunity to come together under one roof to create their designs.

With the blank sculptures delivered to Waterside Mall, an army of artists descended on the studio, selected their blank pandas, mapped out their territory and began passionately bringing their designs to life. For six weeks, the PandaMania studio became a bustling breeding ground for transforming the blank pandas into the colorful creatures that would soon bring plenty of "panda pleasures" to the streets of Washington, D.C.

PANDALA

Artist: **Elizabeth Sworobuk**
Location: **Market Square**

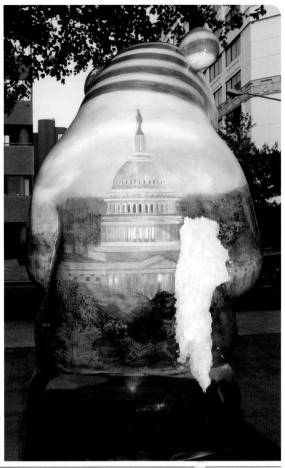

PANDORAMIC WASHINGTON

Artist: **Sharon Roy Finch**
Sponsor & Location: **Embassy Suites Hotel Washington, D.C.**

PANDA ZOODIAC
(Formerly China Zoodiac)

Artist: **Rosemary Luckett**
Sponsor: **Comcast**
Location: **Van Ness/UD.C. Metro Station**

The year 2004 is the "Year of the Monkey" in Chinese astrology. The monkey holding the Chinese yin yang symbol of harmony painted on the front of "Panda Zoodiac" by Rosemary Luckett is a wish for peace during 2004.

PANDA-MONET-UM

Artist: **Cindi Berry**
Sponsor & Location: **Powell, Goldstein, Frazer & Murphy LLP**

"Panda-Monet-um" by Cindi Berry incorporates images from seven paintings by the French impressionist, Claude Monet. Can you name the seven paintings?

CHERRY BLOSSOM

Artist: **Bridget Parris**
Sponsor: **Crabtree + Company**
Location: **Old Post Office Pavilion**

(B)LING-(B)LING

Artist: **Washington Glass Studio**
Sponsor: **Ann Hand**
Location: **Corcoran Gallery of Art**

"(B)ling-(B)ling," created by students and staff at the Washington Glass Studio, was designed with 7,000 pieces of cut, fused and applied glass. Hidden on the sculpture are a flaming heart, a bottle, a fish, a mouse, a monkey, a face and a heart-shaped tattoo. After four tries, the students were able to cast a hat that finally fit their stylish glassy friend.

125

BRAIN STORM

Artist: **Jonathon Lanham**
Location: **International Spy Museum**

PANDART!

Artist: **Raphael Pantalone**
Sponsor & Location: **D.C. Commission on the Arts & Humanities**

E PLURIBUS PANDUM

Artists: **Ferebee Streett Thulman**
Location: **The World Bank**

PANTASY

Artists: **Angela White**
Sponsor & Location: **National Museum of Women in the Arts**

PANDACAMOUFLAGE

Artist: **Caroline Thorington**
Sponsor & Location: **National Museum of Natural History**

There are 45 animals from six continents, including five pandas hidden on "Pandacamouflage" by Caroline Thorington. The artist planned to paint the panda in her studio but the panda preferred the wide-open space of her living room and refused to fit through the studio door. In the end, the panda got its way, staying in the living room where the artist painted it.

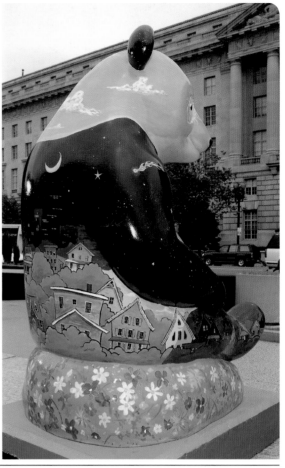

NIGHT AND DAY PANDA

Artist: **John Nickerson**
Sponsor & Location: **National Museum of American History**

THE PANDA'S ZOO

Artist: **Hugo Salinas**
Sponsor & Location: **Mexican Cultural Institute**

PANDAchine

Artist: **Sandie Bacon**
Sponsor & Location: **National Air and Space Museum**

CELADON PANDA

Artist: **Sharon Moody**
Sponsor: **Freer Gallery of Art and Arthur M. Sackler Gallery**
Location: **Smithsonian Castle, Haupt Garden**

"Celadon Panda" by Sharon Moody celebrates Celadon stoneware pottery developed during the Five Dynasties (907-960 C.E.). Called qingci, which means "greenish porcelain," Celadon is highly valued because of its resemblance to jade, China's most precious gemstone.

134

WONDERFUL WORLD

Artist: **Mirta Meltzer**
Location: **Borders Books**

MIRACLE

Artist: **Cornelia Atchley**
Location: **Washington National Cathedral**

CLEAN PANDA

Artist: **Lena Frumin**
Location: **RFK Stadium**

BEYOND THE CHERRY BLOSSOMS

Artist: **Denine Wish**
Sponsor: **D.C. Marriott &
Renaissance Hotels**
Location: **Renaissance Washington, D.C.
Hotel**

PANDA DYNASTY

Artist: **Carol Wood & Regis Kirby**
Sponsor: **Metropolitan Washington Airports Authority**
Location: **Ronald Reagan Washington National Airport**

THE HIKE THAT SAVED THE C & O CANAL

Artist: **Tom Kozar**
Location: **Washington Harbor**

PETER PANDA

Artist: **Melissa Daman**
Sponsor & Location: **Four Seasons Hotel**
Washington, D.C.

139

PLAYING WITH PAINT

Artists: **Hunters Woods Elementary School for Arts and Science Students**
Location: **George Washington University**

PANDAROUND TOWN

Artist: **Jody Bergstresser**
Sponsor: **Comcast**
Location: **City Hall at the Wilson Building**

PANDA PEREGRINATION

Artist: **Renee Alberts**
Location: **Zanzibar Restaurant**

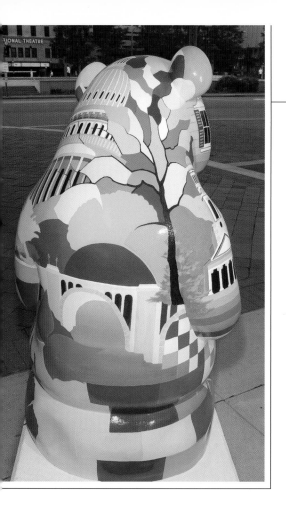

PANDAROUND TOWN

Artist: **Jody Bergstresser**
Sponsor: **Comcast**
Location: **City Hall at the Wilson Building**

PANDA PEREGRINATION

Artist: **Renee Alberts**
Location: **Zanzibar Restaurant**

HONEY POT PANDA

Artists: **Millennium Mind**
Sponsor: **Golden Triangle BID, Corp.**
Location: **Blake Building**

CROUCHING TIGER HIDDEN NIXON

Artist: **Ian Green**
Location: "**The Giant Chair**"

144

BASKING IN THE SUNFLOWERS

Artists: **Marni Maree**
Location: **Starbucks Coffee**

"Basking in the Sunflowers" by Marni Maree came to life in the artist's garage in Springfield, Virginia. "Sunny," as the artist calls him, caused quite a stir while traveling in the back of a pick-up truck to his new home in Washington, D.C.

145

ALICE'S PANDA

Artist: **Patricia Secco**
Sponsor & Location: **Brazilian Embassy in Washington, D.C.**

PANDA IN PARADISE

Artist: **Carla Golembe**
Sponsor: **Discovery Creek Children's Museum of Washington**
Location: **Georgetown Plaza**

HIDE 'N' SEEK

Artist: **Victoria Palley**
Sponsor: **FedSpell**
Location: **Starbucks Coffee**

PANDORA'S PANDA

Artist: **Chary Robbins**
Sponsor: **Capital Hotel and Suites/ St. Gregory Hotel and Governor's House Hotel**
Location: **St. Gregory Hotel**

BAMBOO BEAR I

Artist: **Juan Bernal**
Sponsor: **Washington Metropolitan Area Transit Authority**
Location: **Jackson Graham Building**

BAMBOO BEAR II

Artists: **Carolyn Faulkner**
Sponsor & Location: **The Fairmont**
Washington, D.C.

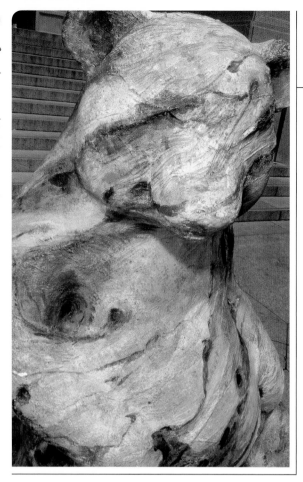

BEARLY DISCERNABLE

Artist: **Wendy Garner**
Sponsor & Location: **National Museum of Natural History**

Panda Population Explosion

THE ROAD TO OBTAINING APPROVALS TO INSTALL THE 150 PandaMania sculptures was arduous and lengthy. As with all art installations on public property, the D.C. Arts Commission is required to obtain permits from District Government. The same is true for public art planned for Federal property, however, permission must come from Federal agencies. The Commission must also receive approvals from property owners to install artwork on private property. Luckily, the Commission learned the path (some would say, cut the path) when it obtained 200 permits to install the donkey and elephant sculptures for Party Animals in 2002.

With permits and approvals in hand, the Arts Commission proceeded with installing 150 panda sculptures in downtown Washington and in District neighborhoods. The Commission, with the help of a professional moving company, installed the pandas over an amazingly short period of five nights. This made the panda's morning appearance seem sudden to pedestrians. Morning after morning, new pandas busted on the scene bringing with them new life and color. The sculptures, like the endearing creatures after which they were modeled, appeared to take great pleasure in their new habitat and the enjoyment of their countless admirers.

THE GARDEN VARIETY PANDA

Artist: **Patricia Leith**
Location: **Benning Road Metro Station**

Giant Panda Hug

...he resounding success of PandaMania is a result of the hard work and dedication of many people who shared the ...C. Arts Commission's vision to bring another exciting art project to the streets of Washington, D.C. The D.C. ...rts Commission thanks everyone who, in small and large ways, contributed to the success of the project. The ...ts Commission especially acknowledges the individuals and organizations listed below for their extraordinary ...ntributions and unwavering support of PandaMania, Washington, D.C.

...ne Kellam, Bertha Hall, Cheryl June, Diane Nichols,
Gail West, Jean Baptiste Demaison,
Jean Baptiste Moussari, Jeff Black, Leslie A. Cohen
and Lou Morse *for their help with the PandaMania
Artists Party*
...ne Marchand *for providing technical assistance to
participating artists*
...gust, Lang & Husak, Inc. *for creating the
PandaMania website*
...ALPRO Group
...avanaugh Press, Inc. *for printing the PandaMania map*
...ark Construction *for providing concrete bases and help
with logistics*
...abtree + Company *for designing the PandaMania map*
...C. Commission on the Arts & Humanities staff,
especially Alec Simpson, Lionell Thomas,
Carolyn Parker, Sherry Schwechten and
Rachel Dickerson
...nbassy of Brazil
...ne Embassy of France
...ne Embassy of the People's Republic of China
...nancial Dynamics Business Communications,
especially Stan Collender, Managing Director
...eishman Hillard, Inc, *for providing expert public
relations services, especially* Martha M. Boudreau,
Annette Larkin, Laurie Ann Ryan and
Mary O'Connor LoJacono
...reenfield Belser ltd *for creating the PandaMania Logo*
...e Falero

Michel Huissmann, Robin Amethyst-Ann Bostic,
Tim Ford and Victoria Palley *for painting the many
sculpture bases*
The National Park Service, *especially* Ric... ...erryman
and Leonard D. Lee
Orange Frazer Press, *especially* Marcy Hawley
Patton Boggs LLP, *especially* Paul Jorgensen and
Deborah M. Lodge
The Scorpions Inc. *for their tremendous patience and
tenacity with delivering all 150 pandas*
Smithsonian's National Zoological Park *where Tian Tian
and Mei Xiang reside*
Washington, DC Convention and Tourism Corporation
Washington Metropolitan Area Transit Authority,
especially the WMATA Board of Directors and the Art
in Transit Program, Michael McBride, Crystal Maden
and Betty J. Wallace
Waterfront Associates LLC/The Kaempfer Company,
especially Charles H. Keher, Steve Nanney and
Maggie Chapman
Watkins Security Agency of D.C., Inc., *especially
security personnel*, Captain Tyrone Williams,
Sergeant Kevin Jackson, Sergeant Carlos Gotay,
Sergeant Valerie Board, Paula Alston,
Arnicia Crawford, Linda Whitaker and
Keyana Lindsey
World Wildlife Fund *for being such an ardent supporter of
the project and for sharing with us its knowledge of
pandas*

PandaMania Sponsors

Index Of PandaMania Artists

Participating PandaMania Schools

Bell Multicultural High School Teresa Ghiglino, Art Teacher, Gary Daniels, Teacher, Students: Doris Alvarado, Jessica Castro, Luis Cedillos, Leslie Cruz, Nancy Cruz, Daniel Desta, Jose Flores, Olga Fuentes, Jose Garcia, Jose Garcia, Barbara Law, Juan Pablo Lopez, Jorge Maldonado, Lucio Marchante, Aristide Martinez, Nebiat Masresha, Mayelin Matos, Ashley McDowell, Janae Monroe, Kieu Trang Nguyen, Christian Patinio, Al-Hasan Rashida, Francisco Reyes, Kristina Rezene, Hevert Rios, Jessica Rivera, Samuel Rodriguez, Eduardo Romero, Cindy Salvador, Yimy Sanchez, Burnis Terrell, Dawie Tesfamichael, Michael Weldetensaya and Lizeth Won

Hunters Woods Elementary School for Arts and Science Lisa Foley and Catherine Germain, Art Teachers, Students: Tasha Babiarz, Mynor Celis, Bryan Crespin, Ava Driscoll, Jen Dussault, Lanxing Fu, Amy Hirabayashi, Waveney Hudlin, Adanma Noni Huria, Pince Jindal, Maggie Morris, Lauren Quast, Jae Sim and Civia Stein

Janney Elementary School Laure Hunter, Teacher Jordan Aluise, Badra Benkreira, Joseph Church, Kelly Crabtree, Steven Duarte, Jophie Frumin, Susanna Howe, Jamaal Jordan, Fatima Lach-Hab, Devante Lampkins, Katrina Main, Chase McCann, Aaron Paige, Lena Pfeiffer, Roslynn Posley, Hannah Quinn, Kiara Ricea, Paul Shumaker, Tori Wilds, Gabrielle Willis, Alix Woodall and Jeromey Wrenn

Kid Power-D.C. Caroline Cleveland and Max Skolnik, Staff, Students: Rodney Austin, Trinette Barclift, Kayanna Carrington, Brian Crawford, Alicia Gaskins, D'Angelo Hernandez, Briana Jackson, Olivia Richardson, Malaysia Seabrooks, Sidney Smith-Simmons and Stefan Smith-Simmons

Patapsco High School and Center for the Arts Bernadine Zienkiewicz, Art Teacher, Students: Nicole Akehurst, Andrew Arciaga, Robert Barrett, Amanda Beatty, Katie Calkins, Shatarra Cook, Georgia Geisser, Sam Georgieff, Katrin Gorham, Candice Hall, Jacob Henry, Robert Hensley, Charles Hoffman, Talbolt Johnson, Hannan Kallman, Farrell Maddox, Marierose Mapanao, Laura Murray, Lynn Palewicz, Pamela Penland, Robin Rodowsky, Jessica Rolfe, Christie Sheridan, Lauren Sigwart, Erin Warren, Mallory White, and Amando Zacharko

Washington Glass Studio Michael Janis, Tim Tate, Tim Erwin Timmers, assisted by: Kristina Bilonick, Diane Cabe, Priscilla Carver, Jim Fleming, Barbara Fleming, Lisa Freda, Jon Gann, Rion Hoffman, Kay Janis, Linnie Kendrick, Justine Light, Joe Moore, Anne Plant, Kerri Sheehan and Alison Sigethy

Washington International School Nancy Totten and Annette Zamula, Art Teachers, Students: Lindsay Bradley, Louise Bruce, Nichols Ginsburg, Lusine Hakobyan, Charlotte Horton, Sacha Ingber, Lenna Jawdat, Catherine Kelly, Sana Khawaja, Tessa Martin, Rosemary Nicholas, Juhani Nyman, Ana Panduric, Anna Pavlitchenko, Tabitha Perkins, Owen Schmidt, Adrienne Thadani, Kael Valere and Leila Wozniak

D.C. Commission on the Arts and Humanities Staff

Anthony Gittens
Executive Director

Alec Simpson
Assistant Director

Lionell Thomas
Legislative and Grants Program Manager

Sherry Schwechten
Art in Public Places Manager

José Dominguez
Special Programs & New Initiatives Manager

Mary Liniger
Arts Education Coordinator

Alexandra J. MacMaster
Program Specialist

Yann Doignon
Program Consultant

Shirin Ghareeb
Executive Assistant

Mary Eckstein
Folk Arts Program Consultant

Christena Hambrick
Art Bank Coordinator

Cecilia Weeks
Office Supervisor

Carolyn Parker
Program Assistant

Chelita Dyson
Ebony Blanks
Receptionist

Dolores Kendrick
District of Columbia Poet Laureate